Dadi

A first friend of life

9 heart shaped lessons to heal, grow
and celebrate life

By Vivek Bhadraa

This is a work of fiction. Names, characters, businesses, places, events and incidents are either products of the author's imagination or used in a fictitious manner. Any resemblance to actual persons, living or dead, or actual events is purely coincidental.

First Edition: February 2026
Printed in India

Printed at:

Typeset in Crimson Pro

ISBN: 978-93-6070-826-9

Cover Design: Prajakta Sawant

STORYMIRROR
Stories that reflect you

Publisher: StoryMirror Infotech Pvt. Ltd.
Unit No-F/705, 7th Floor, Kailas Corporate Lounge,
Veer Savarkar Road, Vikhroli Park Site,
Vikhroli West, Mumbai-400079,
Maharashtra, India.

Web: storymirror.com
Facebook: @storymirror
Twitter: @story_mirror
Instagram: @storymirror
Email: marketing@storymirror.com

To Grandmother —

The laughter in my silence,

The strength in my weakness,

and the love that shaped every story in this book.

Your love continues to live new lives through these pages.

ACKNOWLEDGEMENTS

This book has been shaped not only by my memories, but by the people who stood beside me throughout my journey — on stage, on screen, and in life.

To my family, who gave me the foundation on which I continue to build my dreams — thank you for your patience, faith, and constant support.

To my mother and Dimple, who cared for Babu with a devotion that words cannot capture — your love gave her dignity, comfort, and joy in every season of her life.

To my theatre team, my actors, and every member who helped me bring stories alive on stage — especially through performances like **"Dadi: A First Friend of Life", "Love U Papa", "Ekakshari Mahamantra Maa",** and many more — thank you for trusting my vision and walking with me through countless rehearsals, late nights, and curtain calls.

To my audience — from theatre lovers to film viewers — who supported my work through productions like Bread, Metamorphosis, Meri Pyari Rachna, Ladies First, and Love in Kalimpong. your love fuels everything I do.

To every single person who encouraged me, believed in me, corrected me, challenged me, or simply smiled at me along the way — you are part of this story.

And above all,

To My Grandmother — My First Friend, my silent strength, my forever teacher.

This book is my way of keeping your warmth alive for the world to feel.

Thank you from the depth of my heart.

AUTHOR'S NOTE

Dadi: A First Friend of Life began long before I ever wrote a page.

It began on stage, as a drama.

It began in my childhood, as memories.

And it truly began the day Babu held my hand and unknowingly gave me the first lessons of life.

This book is an emotional extension of my theatre play *"Dadi: A First Friend of Life."*

What started as a stage performance — filled with nostalgia, mischief, laughter, and tears — has now taken form in these pages, allowing me to share Babu's stories with a wider world.

As a filmmaker and theatre artist, I have told many stories — but this one is closest to my heart, because it shaped the man I became.

Grandmother taught me that love can heal, simplicity can inspire, and even silence can teach. She taught me that strength is gentle, forgiveness is powerful, and life is always worth celebrating — even in its imperfections.

Writing this book was not just a creative process; it was a journey back to the moments that moulded me, guided me, and held me. I hope that as you read, you find a piece of your own childhood, your own loved ones, and your own healing within these chapters.

Thank you for opening your heart to this story.

Thank you for letting my Grandmother enter your world.

Additional Note:

This book is an emotional extension of the theatre drama "Dadi: A First Friend of Life," originally written by Shri Jayprakash Santoki, a respected theatre writer from Lalpur, Jamnagar (Gujarat).

I am grateful to Santoki Sir for creating the original dramatic foundation that inspired me years later to turn this story into a book. His writing helped me relive Babu's memories in a deeper way, and it is an honor to acknowledge his contribution in this journey.

— Vivek Bhadraa

TABLE OF CONTENTS

THE CELEBRATION OF LIFE..........11

A FIRE WITHIN NANBAI..........29

DREAMS UNSPOKEN..........33

RELOCATION OF PLACE AND THOUGHTS..........45

BIG HEART..........51

FAITH..........63

POSITIVE TEACHING..........75

FASHION MODEL BABU..........81

FINAL MOMENTS: HES LAST LESSON OF LOVE..........87

Chapter

ONE

THE CELEBRATION OF LIFE

Introduction of Nanbai and the people around her. How she takes care of her loved ones and how she is treated.

Her life and problems from the point of view of her grandson.

Whenever I think of her, the word “Celebration of life” comes to my mind. Always happy and smiling. The ever-burning flame of positivity and the leader of mischief in our family.

Nanba, my grandmother, was the youngest soul in our whole family. My sister Dimple, my mother, and I used to call her “Babu”. She was different in all the aspects one expects of an old lady.

When we picture a grandmother, we see a grey-haired old woman in spectacles, a smiling wrinkled face with faded charm. We see someone sitting in a corner doing meditation or sitting outside the house sharing their lifelong pain with her like-minded friends.

Babu was beautiful. People used to call her NRI Dadi due to her fair and charming complexion. Nonetheless, she used to treat herself like a princess. The moment she entered the room, she either brought positivity or laughter. Telling some stupid jokes or playing pranks was her mastery. She behaved like the lady of the big house, giving us long lectures, asking us to behave and avoid mischief. The moment we were alone, she used to make that puppy face to get back in the team. If a piece of chocolate or a sweet was missing, we knew who it would be.

On the other hand, she was a very firm and devoted person. She was an inspiration to our neighbourhood and other elderly people. She knew everything. She knew everything: home remedies, rituals, recipes, tips and tricks, and what not. Even if one of our neighbours asked her to interview the boy or meet the girl before they said yes for marriage. She had those keen eyes. sparkling like a lake in a winter noon. It was hard for her to be sad and low in energy. Even if she was sitting alone in a chair, she would sing herself a song or take my comic book and look at the pictures figuring out the story.

She did not receive formal education but the knowledge she gained from life was rare, which you cannot find in books somehow.

If an infant child is crying continuously or someone has broken their ankle, has added extra salt to the pickle or is stuck in a critical social situation, unable to see the good things yet still hoping. She was the one those people would have liked to turn to.

Her life was an example to me about one's true connection with the universe. She always saw the good in life and made the most of whatever she had received. She learned from her mistakes and took initiatives.

Whether it is about being helpful to others or putting our faith in the universe, I could feel that she was able to see the things happening around from all perspectives. That can be one of the reasons why I never saw her complaining about anything in her life. I wished to see the world from her eyes and in a way, I did.

While growing up and getting experiences from the outer world, the seeds she planted in us started sprouting. Sometimes even sitting alone I laugh at her childlike talks filled with deep lessons that came from the experiences she gained from her dramatic life.

I was fascinated with the way of living and loved her wholeheartedly but that never meant that I would let go of my rights to tease her and play pranks on her as she was my first best friend. These pranks included making faces and weird noises to tease her, switching off the lights and running away, hanging on her legs if she was going out or disturbing her while on some serious conversation with neighbours.

Calling her just like that to get a reply from her was one of my most favourite activities back then.

"Listen, Babu. Come look at this"

"What?"

“Come and look.” I had to keep my face serious while she got up and walked to me.

“What is it?” She used to come to me and scan the view outside the window with the hope of finding something peculiar.

“What is it, Vivek? I cannot see anything.” Her curiosity took over.

“Look. The sky!” I pointed at the sky.

“Where? What is it with the sky? I cannot see anything there...” She squinted her eyes.

“It is as blue as it was yesterday...” I smirked and shot away.

“Oh. Yes.” Upon the realization of being fooled again, she used to rush after me. “I will remember this and you will not be forgiven for this. Do you need a scolding?” But by the time she tried to catch me, I was long gone from her reach.

“Come back. I will teach you a lesson.” Getting back the sweet revenge and evening the score was one of our daily agendas.

I was indeed mischievous. Being the first child in the family has its own pros and cons. Being the first is good because you get all the princely attention and luxuries, but soon you will be the eldest one who will be responsible for taking care of the new member. When I engaged in mischief, I came back home with broken bones or a punctured “Chako” (I named my bicycle “Chako”), and I was the subject of complaints from school.

However, I was not the only mischievous one, and that kept me safe and protected. “Babu” was my partner in crime, my mentor, and my best friend.

She possessed the best childlike innocent smile ever given. I even asked her if she wanted me to call her "Dadimaa" or "Baa", and she replied while folding the clothes one by one from a huge mound of washed clothes in front of her, "Nope."

"But you are my grandmother, so..." I pushed a little.

"Should I start calling you a Monkey? As we know, you are a monkey with a missing tail." She chuckled.

"Yes. You are right. I will call you "Babu" then." I would have escalated it to tease her more but I accepted my defeat instantly.

"You can call me with whatever name or word you feel suitable for me. Your love matters to me, not the name."

She looked at me.

I always saw her smiling, occupied with some work, gardening, chopping the vegetables, making flower garlands, cooking something special for us, cleaning the yard, or helping someone. She was famous in our neighbourhood for her "Grandmaa's tips" and her helpful nature and infectious smile.

If someone is sick or wants to make some rare dish, rituals for Vrat or homemade remedies, people know whom to approach. She loved talking to people, asking about their life, making them feel cared for and easing them up as if they were her own. Also, she never projected her knowledge or thoughts on anyone. She was a free-spirited bird.

"We should help others. Help does not mean only when you give them money or go work for them. Sometimes, just listening to them and giving them a little smile infused

with hope and positivity is also a big help," she used to say. "Remember that there are people who can help and there are people who are in need of help. Being capable of helping someone is a blessing." Her ideology did not come from any book or lectures. It came from her childhood and life that she gave everything to build for her kids.

Sometimes I wonder how someone can be so giving, loving, caring for everyone?

How can someone give all the credit to others, remain detached and yet live a wonderful life with such ease? How can one possess the art of becoming the person one is with and helping them out in one's own way? "May she be a magician," my young brain also brought these thoughts.

Well, one of the most magical and remarkable qualities that defined her was her ability to find joy and gratitude in the simplest of things. Isn't it cool? She was a walking epitome of positivity and kindness.

She knew how to create magical moments for us and turn our boring hot summer days into wonderful adventurous trips. She would tell ghost stories or cook sweets especially for us, buy new clothes or give us magical lessons wrapped in exciting incidents, make us laugh by mimicking grandpa or save us from the punishment for the mischief we had performed. She always made sure that we ate right, did our homework on time, played enough and stayed away from that brown dog in the 3rd lane. That dog liked to chase little kids and also bit a few.

At a certain age, I understood that kids have a different set of eyes when it comes to measuring things happening around the world. Kids always try to shorten things to adjust to their own understanding about the world. On a great note she was an old grandmother, the lady of the house, someone who is more responsible and has seen the ups and downs of life. While for me, she was someone with childlike talks, dreams, a positive way to look at life and a craving to enjoy every moment at hand.

I never liked it when someone raised their voice to her or someone did something which sets her mood off temporarily.

Especially, my grandfather was often the one to do so. He was a man with anger and authority in the house. I was not able to understand what was wrong with him or what caused him to be so mad at Babu. I thought that she should take a break from that annoyance, anger, or the warrior mode for once. He can laugh with others, help people, give advice even if they are not required, but when it comes to Babu, his attitude remains the same.

I still remember the day I was doing my homework and heard his voice. I initially thought that someone might have stepped on his toe, so I rushed to check. There he was scolding Babu for something I don't remember. "Is this tea or sugar-syrup?" he roared with a low yet deadly tone. "You know I do not like sweet tea. Make me strong masala tea." Babu nodded and vanished in the kitchen preparing tea for him again because Dadaji was talking to himself. "Even at this age there is no development in your brain. "Same old stupid face and work." He gave a disappointed look at me.

How many times have I asked everyone not to add any sugar in my tea or food. But who cares? Within a minute, Babu came back with another cup of hot masala chai.

"How is it?" Babu inquired and he did not even reply.

Before Nanbai replies, someone from the kitchen intervened, "I prepared the tea , Bapuji, and she had no idea that I added sugar in it."

"Had no idea? Was it my fault? And... Where was he busy? After roaming the whole world to meet our requirements, when a man comes home tired, what does he ask for? A cup of good tea. Not much.

She cannot do that simple thing right, either." The fire-breathing dragon looked at her while sipping the masala chai.

"For your age, it is not good to get angry. Your BP will rise again," my mother tried to calm him down. "Drink tea before it gets cold." And this further fueled his anger.

"My whole life is cold. I wish to die rather than live this life. How can someone be so irresponsible after so many years? My whole life became a joke also. You have no knowledge at all. Just cooking and cleaning, nothing more." He kept the teacup on the table and started rocking back and forth in his chair.

"Where did she go?" He looked at my mother again.

"In the backyard."

"Call her here."

"Leave it, Bapuji. You enjoy your tea. If you need something, tell me; I will get it done."

"Did she press my clothes for tomorrow's trip?"

"All clothes were washed and ironed only yesterday," Nanbai replied humbly.

“Which ones?”

“Those white Kurtas, pants, and Koti”

“And the new pair which I purchased from the old market last month?”

“That one had a little yellow mark on it from the curry someone spilled on you that day”

“One simple Kurta you cannot clean for God’s sake. You are doing this knowingly to humiliate.”

“We all tried. You can put the Koti on it; it will not be visible,” she innocently suggested.

“Wow. Use your brain more than you use your people. People, wow, know this is good and I am lucky. This is what my luck looks like” he shot another missile at Babu.

I do not know what intense thoughts engulfed him but with a quick movement he got up and walked out fuming. It was not much but it was intense.

At this point, I wish he had remained outside only. I just wanted to go to the backyard and sit with Babu where she was occupied with other work.

An hour passed and nothing happened. Dadaji went outside for his business and Babu was busy in the backyard. I wanted to go to her, talk to her but I thought, what will I tell her? Is there anything I can do for her?

It was strange for me that everyone else was silent and did nothing about it. In the evening she came and went into the kitchen and started cooking. One by one the whole family sat and had their dinner. My heart started pounding when

Dadaji came and sat. Babu came with a well-prepared plate for him. It looked special to me. Huge plate with roti, sabji, butter, fried chili, buttermilk, and more.

I looked at him and smiled faintly. "Eat silently and do not say anything, otherwise I will hit you with something now."

I was so sick from the inside, so I refused to eat.

"I am not feeling well. Maybe I will eat later" I lied.

"What happened to you dear? Did you eat anything from outside?" before even thinking ahead, Babu spoke.

"Nope. I am not hungry" I made that "not so happy" face to her.

"Do you want to eat something else my dear"

"No issue. Eat later. Now go and take rest if you are not good" Babu motioned to me to go and rest.

I went up to the terrace from the stairs in the backyard and lay on the bed. Everything was bothering me: Dadaji's voice, the silence of everyone, and Babu's pain and helplessness.

How can this be? She does not deserve to be treated this way. Why?

With each thought warm tears were rolling from my eyes.

Before I could wipe my tears, she came, as good as new, with the same energetic voice and life.

How is this possible? I thought to myself: She was being insulted in front of the whole house a few hours ago, was called names and now I heard her calling my name with the same energy and spark.

When I refused to reply, she came to me and sat beside my bed.

“Come. I have prepared your favourite food: Kheer, Puri, and potato sabji with no chili.”

“I am not hungry. I will not eat. You go.”

“Oh, this attitude! Why? What have I done now?” She made her little princess face to charm me again.

“I told you I am not hungry. Go. Go and give masala chai you like. Right?”

She looked at me and laughed and hugged me.

“Oh la la. You are still there. It is okay. Relax, she likes that. She’s always angry. God also hides when he visits the temple, you know. He was angry over his tea and that the barber did not cut his moustache in the way he liked. So, he took it out here. That’s all.”

Why did you not argue? Tell him to prepare his own tea and if he wishes he can add his tobacco in that also.”

“This much anger. Anger consumes our energy and our body needs energy to work and be happy.”

“So, she needed to be happy.” I intervened.

She paused for a moment. “Come on. Let’s go and have dinner. I am also very hungry. If you are not eating, I am also skipping the dinner today.”

“No, I will eat now. Come on. I am hungry.” I got up from the bed and went to the stairs waiting for her to follow me.

She got up and soon I was sitting beside her outside the kitchen and was served with my favourite meal. I now know that the Kheer was not sweet at all. It was only her love and charm that made it mind-blowing.

A while ago people were busy in their own lives but as long as I was having my favourite dish, everyone came out from their hibernation.

"Is he eating food with no chili again? From tomorrow he is eating whatever is given on the plate. I do not tolerate this." I never cussed in my life but from that point I understood how you feel when you cuss someone. Yet, having Babu on my side, I was relaxed.

"He does not feel well when he eats chili. Once he had something spicy and that is why his stomach was upset." She made up something quickly.

"From tomorrow he is eating with others and he is eating whatever is given."

"Sure. He will. Gautamji's son came asking for you for a few minutes. They are starting the meeting early." Babu informed Dadaji in a casual manner.

"Why did you not tell me before? Now I have to get ready." Talking to himself and cussing someone we could not even see, he went back to his room to get ready.

I looked at Babu and gave her a sharp fiery look, "I do not like this. Any of them. Why do you still do what they say and be nice to them? Get angry and shout and say I will not do it. I will help you with that. It will be fun. We will teach them a lesson. Do not wash the clothes, do not make tea. Hide somewhere. He will prepare it himself."

It was hard for her to hold back her laughter, "Sounds nice. It will be fun for sure but where should I hide and for how long and what if no one comes and finds me?"

"Are you listening to me Babu, do not make fun of me. Please." I pleaded with her to be rebellious.

She first laughed a lot and it took a while for her to catch her breath and replied, "Are you willing to stay hungry little monster? I am the queen of the house and sometimes if he gets angry and relaxes, let him be. Ultimately we are the ones who rule the house." She blinked at me. On the other hand if he really gets upset and gets me out of the house, where will I go at this age? Oh God. No. I do not want to get kicked out of the house and roam here and there. I am good here. Once you grow up, build a super house and make me the queen. I will come and stay there with you and you will treat me as a queen."

I suddenly was taken from my furious rebellious talks to a magical land.

"Yes, I will make a big house with big rooms and good kitchen and servants and all facilities. It will be just you and me and ma, papa and Dimple. No one else will enter." I took a deep breath of excitement "and there will be a special room for you and in my house you will not work. You will give orders and people will come and do as you command and we will not invite Dadaji there." I whispered cautiously.

"Oh, my! Why is that? He is your grandfather after all." She stopped what she was doing and looked at me seriously.

"Because he shouts at you and cusses you and always insults you. I will buy a dog. I will buy many dogs instead and will train them to chase him away and tear his clothes and chase him till he leaves the town," I chuckled maniacally.

She laughed so hard that people who were busy with their own agendas had to take a glance at the event.

"What happened?" Dadaji came out and was putting his shoes on, and intervened with his years-long authority.

"Nothing, just a silly thing. Not much," She answered with ease. "No wonder. Fits you. Keep it down. I do not think you are going to the meeting now." Grandpa taunted her, his words like loud noises in my house.

"Sure, I will.

I am just going to the backyard for cleaning. Good luck with the dog chasing you," She looked at me and chuckled. We both looked at each other and rushed to the backyard with the plates in which I had completed my dinner.

Chapter TWO

A FIRE WITHIN NANBAI

Nanbai's childhood and struggles, along with her development of a positive approach towards life through attending Bhagvat Katha and Vrat Kathas in the neighbourhood and learning about how to be happy, are central themes. Self-taught Nanbai makes her way towards living a positive life.

Along the coast of the Gulf of Kutch, there is a small town named Sandhan. That is where she was born 85 years ago and even without doing anything she brought momentary joy and long disappointment to her orthodox family. The reason is that the family was longing for a son to carry on the family name and become the head of the family in the future and run the family.

Isn't it strange that without even knowing or doing anything she was marked as a burden in the house? Her curious or hopeful childhood was to be filled with neglect and deprivation.

From a very early age, she became the maid in her own house, cleaning, cooking, running errands, helping on the farm, running back home, cooking, and cleaning. She would sleep after all work was done, wake up before everyone else, and get back to the time loop again.

However, in her own words, she had a "wonderful" childhood. Yes, I also felt that she was crazy when she said so. Diving deep in her memories, her eyes always sparkled. "I was fast and people loved that about me, whether cleaning the house, delivering the tiffin at the farm, or washing the clothes. When I am on it, it will be done in just a few minutes. I loved my work and especially loved festivals. Everything was so energetic and happening. People get new clothes, sweets, and visits from their relatives, and if you are lucky, someone will also hand you a penny. I used to hand it to my mother as she would use it for family expenses."

At one point, she understood that her own happiness lies within her as everyone around her either wants her to work or take care of all the responsibilities. She was from her family and was taught to endure the hardships of life without making complaints. But it was she who decided to keep her high spirits alive.

In a time when basic education was also considered a luxury reserved for the privileged few, Nanbai was denied the opportunity to read, write, or nurture her intellect. Her dreams, skills, potential, or willingness were stifled by the walls of illiteracy.

For that, she also had a different view. "I wanted to become a boy when I was a kid. They can go anywhere, play the whole day, attend school, and go outside and come back home even after evening. Even in marriage, they are the ones who get to dress well, sit on the horse, and dance. Girls were crying at their own wedding."

A fire within Nanbai was alive with all her positivity of living life beautifully and the positivity of fighting with all the hurdles in her life. She moved on and had hope and belief in God's plan for her.

Chapter THREE

DREAMS UNSPOKEN

In one corner of her heart, she preserved a dream of her dream life and a dream home, where she will be treated with love and care, and where she will be able to speak and sing and dance and laugh and celebrate and go out and above all receive the love she always looked for.

When we are kids, what mostly consumes our thoughts is what we will do next, which candy we will buy next or when the next fun-fair is coming to the town. We crave sweets and playing video games. We make sure to jump into the little puddle in the middle of the ground in monsoon, to make slides with blankets in winters. Taking mental notes of when the kulfiwala comes and where he stands to see him. It is the age of adventure and mischief, the age of growth and fun. At night we dream about how our superhero will get out of the carnivorous forest he landed in.

Maybe not for everyone. When I see little kids doing hard work to earn a piece of bread and butter, compromising their dreams to help their family, or living in a grey, emotionless world where they are seen only as a working force or apprentices, I see eyes whose dreams are faded and a guilty-filled smile. They are guilty of their own existence.

Things were not different for Babu either. At the very fragile age of 15 she got married to a man 15 years older than her. She had not started to understand the world, apart from working hard to be of some help for her impoverished family. She was not mature enough to understand that now her life is about to take a dramatic turn.

"I was excited and also embarrassed. My dulha was a big man but I was happy. Many of my friends also got married and it was my turn now. I felt so happy that I would get new clothes and jewellery, and our relatives and my friends would come home just for me. They would apply mehndi on my hands. Everyone would sing wedding songs with playful teasing and my dulha's name in them. I would make fun of it. I felt like a princess at that time. The only thing I had to do was to remain serious and not speak or look at anyone. Just nod and do as I was told." She sighed. "We would go to a new town, away from my parents, and we would live in a new house and start a new life. Maybe I would get a chance to get a ride on a scooter, a bus, or, if I was lucky, in a car. That was so exciting. I kept dreaming about what I would do in my life and that I would do them all."

Her innocence and gratitude came from the pain and struggles she endured in her life. The flame burning from the core is hard to put out. It always comes back to life.

I still wonder about one's perception, maturity, and awareness of oneself. Whether it was the little girl or the parents who were unaware of their actions. Many of them were like this when these things were considered common in society.

Surprisingly, with her husband she felt just like home. The only change was that now she was under the burden of responsibilities which she sometimes did not know how to handle. They had to go to Jamnagar, where they lived in a very small room as their new home.

Now she was subordinate to someone else and had to follow instructions without questions or complaints. On top of that my Dadaji was a rough man. He was a master at giving lectures, shouting and cussing. Constant taunts, complaints, and occasionally beating scared her soul.

It must have been hard for her to understand whether she was part of the family or was a war prisoner.

Considering it as a birthright of a man, Dadaji rarely missed a chance of giving her lectures or collective insults.

She had to wake up early, clean the house, get ready, make breakfast and masala chai for my dadaji and wash clothes and other household tasks. Her energy and excitement for her new life became fatigued in no time.

As a little girl, she needed someone to talk to, share things, to ask questions and to appreciate things.

Someone with whom she could feel safe. But she had a fear of judgments or of being verbally insulted when she faced her fair share of questions in the initial days.

Her husband, a rough, confident soul with coarse laughing outbursts and with thundering tongue, had never recognised the strength and the grace that radiated from her. At the age when someone starts developing their personality and understands their worth, Nanbai was losing hers.

She was burdened with immense responsibilities, both within her household and outside.

This could have turned into a sad, melodramatic story we hear every now and then where the victim lives a sacrificial life and gives everything away, tolerates mistreatment, creates a chain of events throughout her life by passing on the same pain to the next generation.

Babu was not one of them. She soon realized that this was it and from this she had to make a wonderful life for herself. The emotional urges and rough life moved her towards spirituality and God. She, in no time, started attending the pravachans in the neighbourhood. Listening to devotional stories and Bhagavad Gita empowered her soul once again.

"You must have cried a lot Babu, feeling alone, scared, and unsafe? What will you do in this life and how will you manage things in the future?" I asked her one day when I fell from my bicycle and broke my knee.

"Why would I? Yes, I felt bad and devastated at one point but never helpless. What I understood from life is that I was sent on Earth for a reason. Where I was, what was happening in my life, and the lessons I was learning are there for a purpose.

God is not mad at me or anyone else. He was there with me and is with me now. I have accepted life."

"So you surrendered to the situation, gave up on hope?" I jumped in between.

"Lala, accepting and giving up are different."

"Okay. Explain, please, Deviji."

"When Mata Sita was abducted by Ravana, she accepted it. She did not surrender. She accepted that she had to be there until Lord Rama came and rescued her. She knew her decision and what she had to go through, the pain, the threats, the mind games by Ravana and his female guards. She would have to stand her ground and have trust in the divine force to help her. not questioning and crying, 'Why did this happen to me?' 'Why did I have to suffer for Vanvaas?' 'Why did I have to live in the forest with no luxuries I deserve?' 'Or why did Ravana have to come and kidnap me?' 'What will he do now?' 'Should I think about what Ravana is saying?' 'Should I wait for Lord Rama, and will he come and rescue me, which seems impossible as they do not even know where I am?' 'They do not have the directions, the support, or the army to fight Ravana and rescue me.' 'There are no boats that they can sail here to find me.' 'The monsters here are 10 times bigger than humans.' 'If they wish, they can eat me in a bite.' What did they do to Rama and Lakshmana?' She took a moment to catch her breath.

"Then... What did she do. Come on tell me quickly." I was now waiting in the story for her to show me what happened next?

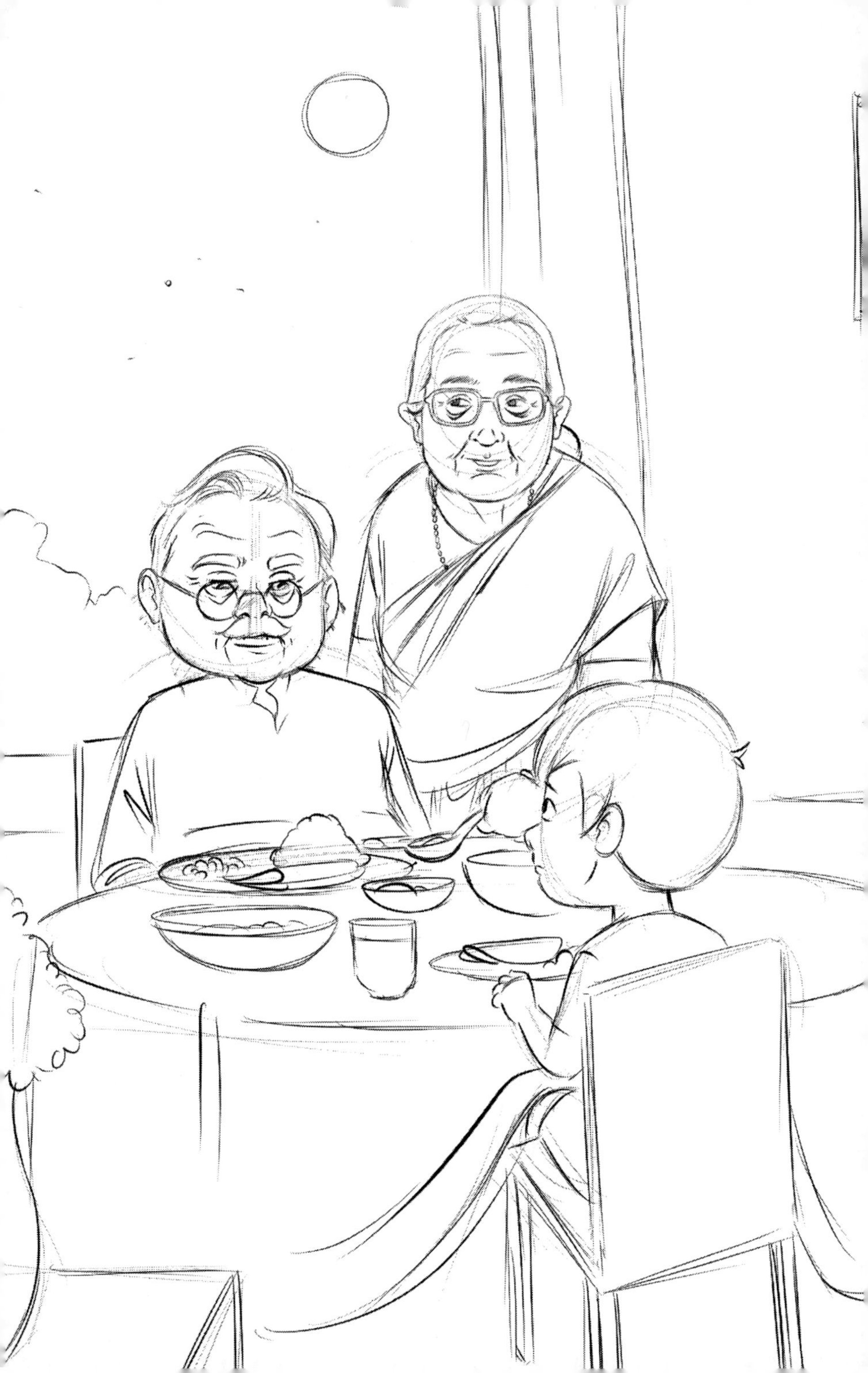

She chuckled again. “She did not panic. She kept her faith in the divine plan intact. She was not afraid, impatient, or weak, not listening to any doubt-inducing rumors from those guards about what would happen to her if she did not listen to Ravana. She accepted that she was in a situation and that her decision and response would change the fate of many lives going forward. She remained there fearless, content, and with grace. Nothing could shock her dignity or purity. Among all the demons and monsters, she was the most powerful being they ever saw. It was her faith in Lord Rama, the faith in her love, and the faith that whatever was happening was happening for a reason that kept the flame alive.”

“So what happened to her then? Did Ram sneak into Lanka secretly and rescue her before anyone could spot him?” I added my own version of the story.

“Nope. He did not.” She nodded with sadness in her tone.

“Ohh. It is obvious. There was no way he could do it. No news, no direction, no army, no roads, and no help.” I reached the conclusion of a sad story.

“Do you know what happened next?”

“Ravana killed Sita and the monsters ate her?” Hopelessly angry, I replied.

“Nope. Meanwhile, Rama was determined to find Sita and as soon as he knew Sita was in danger, he and Lakshmana decided to find her and rescue her. One by one they met people, allies, and friends and help started coming in from every direction they knew. There was a young prince named Ram who is on a quest to save his wife Sita from Ravana. Whoever heard this rushed to him, offering their help in whatever way possible.”

"But was not Rama a god? Cannot he go and confront Ravana and scold him, beat him, and rescue Sita at once?"

"Then why would he need us? Everyone in his story had a role to play: a credit to take, and a task to be part of a divine plan."

"Ohhh. Then..."

"Then with the help of every living being on their way, they built a bridge over the sea to Lanka and fought Ravan and rescued Sita."

"Wow...that sounds so heroic! Rama must be powerful and undefeatable..."

"He was for sure. So did Mata Sita and so did Ravan. If he wished, he could have ended the war before it even started, Sita, if she wished, could have done it by herself, she was Devi herself. But here, it was not personal. It was universal. Ravana caused pain and riots for so many lives. His chaos was to be put to an end..."

"...does it mean that he only acted when his own wife was in danger, otherwise, why did he not act before that? Was he selfish, that he did not act before?"

"He came here in a human form. To teach a lesson that things can go wrong in anyone's life, whether humans or gods. You have to take action and not cower away in desperation and cry, but you have to take steps ahead and understand the divine plan and your importance in it. He received help from giant monkeys to little birds and squirrels also helped. Even God cannot help. But if you decide to get up and fight back, every bit of positive energy and help will come your way and find you."

"Hmm?"

"He taught us to be sure of ourselves. Know your worth and have faith that whatever happens is for a reason. Whether you can see it or not. That is life. If God wishes us to face things, we are mere humans. Standing upright, facing the obstacles, and making our way out without losing hope or our morals is what one should do."

"And you kept faith in yourself and God."

"I did. I had to. And I am glad about it. I feel good when I see my family happy and content, struggling but not giving up, and earning less but living a confident and moral life."

Chapter FOUR

RELOCATION OF PLACE AND THOUGHTS

Relocating to Jamnagar City in Gujarat with her husband, Nanbai devoted herself to her family and her faith, seeking solace in the spiritual teachings and Kathas (pravachan) of God. Soon, she embraced motherhood, giving birth to her first child at the tender age of 16. However, the joy was fleeting as fate dealt a cruel blow—her firstborn passed away before reaching the age of two. At that time, many years ago, there weren't proper medical facilities, so her child didn't get proper treatment. It was a very sad moment in the house. Everyone knew that this was a very great loss, but in those olden times, people didn't care much for mothers as they do in the present time. As you know, Nanbai was also left alone in this so-called dark condition.

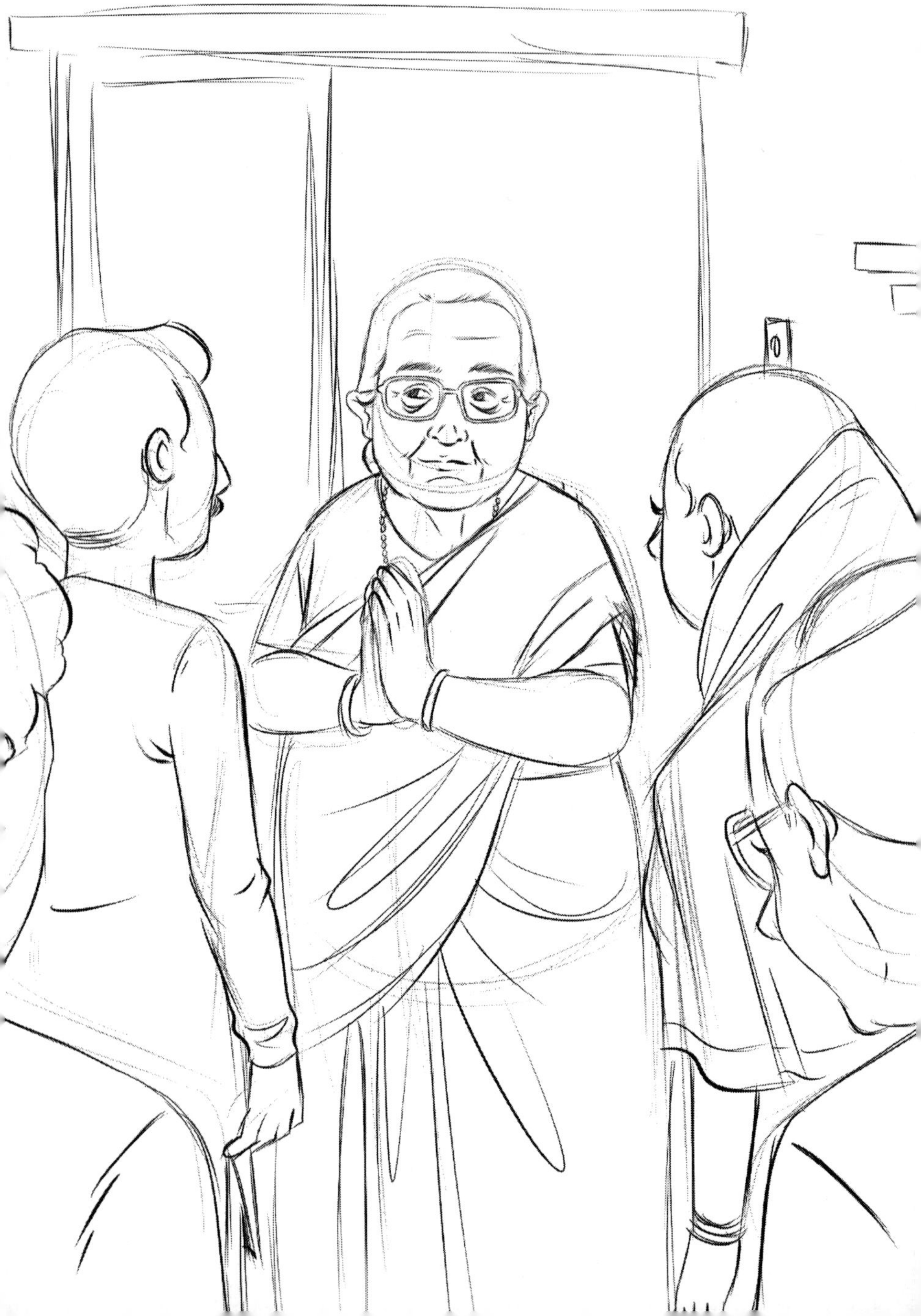

The loss of her child shattered Nanbai's heart, yet she summoned an immense inner strength to rebuild her shattered world. Behind her infectious smile, she concealed the depths of her pain, never burdening others with her sorrows. Instead, Nanbai dedicated herself to instilling innocence and goodness in every one of her children, imparting invaluable life lessons and the importance of embracing humanity.

She relocated her thoughts and moved further in her life. After this incident, she became more positive and came to know how she had to battle in this world. She did all the things that came to her mind. She learned how to live life accordingly. After all this battle she gave birth to 5 children back to back among whom the eldest were two daughters named Rekha and Shanti. After that God gifted her with three kings, her three sons named Ishwar, Jayanti, and Chandrakant.

I would not expand the story as it will be a bit boring for all. So I will cut the story short and say that, among all these children, remember the name Jayanti, as Jayanti got married to a beautiful girl named Neeta, after their marriage completed its second year, Neeta gave birth to a child named Vivek, who is me. After that I got a beautiful cute little sister named Dimple.

From here Nanbai's new chapter has started as we were her favorites. Remember Neeta, my mom, Dimple, my sister, and I, Vivek. We three were her favorites. As I have other sisters too, my dad's brother named Chandrakant has two daughters named Riya and Mona. My father's elder brother Ishwar also has two children named Jitu and Darshana.

We are not deep diving into this family tree and we will start with very shortly from here. The story will continue from my side. Vivek, I'm narrating the full story of my grandmother, my best friend, the first friend of my life, my grandma Nanbai 'Babu'.

Chapter FIVE

BIG HEART

The world is a very strange place. Especially for those who are yet to explore it. Kids, to be precise.

Being the eldest kid of the family, I felt that I was the king and that I was entitled to do anything I wish. I remember my parents talking about my education, taking my demands seriously and giving me good attention. Even Dadaji never got angry with me for my little mischief. Considering love and care as my birthright, I was flying. I used to ride my bicycle on the narrow streets like an arrow reaching the target, I looked at people as if they did not matter to the world. At one point, I felt that everything should go around as I wish.

However, Spoiled as I was, I used to come home with broken bones, ripped clothes, complaints from people and blood dripping from my forehead or grazed skin on my hand.

Things were going smoothly until one day I changed my idea of things.

I loved my bicycle so much that I named it 'Chako,' which means a small twittering bird.

It was the precious gem of my life. I loved it so much that I used to dream of myself riding it on an empty street made of white marble. I loved to ring its bell to make people aware of my arrival and step aside. I used to keep it clean and decorate it on every occasion.

I even used to introduce our guests to it.

One day, I was riding it towards someone's house to deliver something my mother gave me. I was happily riding it and enjoying each pedal stroke. When I stopped at a shop to buy something, a boy looked at my bicycle and started touching it. Well, I usually had good terms with most of the people in the neighbourhood. But here, someone whom I barely knew was touching my bicycle. He was ringing the bell, jiggling the handlebar, and kicking the pedal. I got down and asked him to stop it and stay away from it.

Whether he did not hear it or ignored it, he continued. I stepped closer and repeated the same thing. He stepped away. The moment I went back to the shop counter, he went near the bicycle and kicked it hard, jumped on it and ran away with the other kids.

I knew I could run so fast, and that I also had a beast side.

I do not remember what happened next but I was now standing in front of my house with scratched knees, grazed elbows, dirty fists and ripped shirts.

My mother noticed me and rushed to me. Looking at me and my devastated condition, she started inquiring and scolding me.

"What have you done? Why is there not a single day when you come home peacefully? There's always something new. What did you do this time?"

I explained to her but it did not help.

Babu rushed to me and without saying anything, took me to the bathroom, dressed my wounds, washed my face, hands, and legs. I made sure that I was not hurt anywhere else while applying haldi paste on my wounds.

"What did you do?"

"Nothing"

"I know. Nothing happens when you do nothing. Tell me now so I can work out what to do"

After listening to me she said, 'Is that boy all right?' Did you hit him hard? Was he bleeding?

At that time it was hard for me to digest that she was worried about the boy who mistreated me, fought with me and insulted my bicycle. I got irritated for a while.

Within an hour or so, I heard some noise. It seemed as if so many people were talking loudly to each other. I peeped out from the window to find that the boy, his parents, Mukhi Bapa and a few other people were standing outside with some serious matter at hand.

As a very innocent boy, I had no idea what the matter could be.

I saw my parents standing outside, trying to talk things out, and apologizing for what I did. I heard that in the fight I broke that kid's tooth and he was also injured, as I was.

While inside, I started arguing with Babu that it was not my fault and that the boy was being nonsensical.

She looked at me and said, "I am not asking you about that boy. You also were equally involved in it. Promise me that this is the last time and you will not repeat anything like this in the future."

"But why should I, Babu? He is...."

She took a deep breath and asked again "Are you sure you will not apologize?"

"Nope," I snorted.

"Okay then. No issue."

She walked to the door, stood there and politely apologized for what I did and assured them that I will not repeat anything like this in the future. But I also got a word from them that their son also has to make sure not to bother me again.

Once they were gone, I was the center of attention for everyone. But she took all the blame and received enough blame for me. I was feeling bad as people blamed her for spoiling me and that I were not even listening to her.

At one point, my father got so angry that he shouted my name and called me out.

He had enough of my mischief and could have given it to me but it was Babu who stood beside me. If it was not for her protection, I could have got a good lashing that day.

I was feeling bad on the inside. Not for me. But for her. She did not speak to me for a day. Still taking care of my lunch box and ironed clothes for school, she avoided talking to me.

After a few days of retrospection and self-talk, I understood how spoilt and arrogant I became. It was the absence of Babu's energy in my life that made me understand where I was.

As soon as the school bell rang, I rushed to that boy's home. He was there helping his father with something. He was wearing the same shirt that had ripped on that day. His eyes looked empty and hopeless. Their house was even smaller than ours and in bad condition. Broken walls with peeling paint, doors hardly dangling from the walls, a small yard and nothing more. In a corner, I saw a very old skeleton of what could have been a bicycle ages ago.

His father was angrily shouting at him for something.

My heart was pounding and I thought they would grab me by my arm, drag me in and beat black and blue. I was about to run.

The boy stood up and said, "Do you need anything?"

"No. I came here to apologize. I am sorry for that day."

He opened his mouth and pointed me toward a square gap between two teeth. "That is okay."

"I am really sorry. I..." The heaviness in my heart choked any words coming from my mouth.

"That is okay. Go now."

"Would you like to have a ride?" I offered politely with a worried smile.

"Sure, not today but sure." He smiled back.

Upon going back home, I saw Babu was helping my mother in the kitchen. I just rushed to her, hugged her and cried my heart out. I still do not understand what that was.

She thought that I must have done something or that I might have seen a ghost instead.

When I caught my breath, she took me to the backyard, away from everyone else and asked

"What happened? Did anyone scold you? School teacher? Dadaji? Your father? Anyone else?"

"That boy..."

"Which boy?" She scanned the past and understood what I was talking about.

I explained to her about my visit, my apologies, and his situation. Babu hugged me back and calmed me down.

After a few days, I took one of my new shirts and gave it to him as a peace offering. Initially he and his father denied it, but from the look of my guilt and realization, they accepted it.

With one fight I have damaged my connection with Babu, my childhood friend, and with one apology, I have added one more friend to my life.

Sometimes being kind and taking initiative to apologize makes a huge difference.

Equally, understanding and forgiving someone also requires a big heart.

Chapter SIX

FAITH

There comes a time in everyone's life when things do not turn out the way you wished for. When you struggle with yourself. You doubt your sanity, your skills, and your dreams. When your heart feels stifled and your brain is oozing with tangled thoughts. At one point you were energetic, willing to work, ready to show the world your caliber. On the other side, you did not have any direction where to go, whom to ask, what to do, and how to get hold of your life.

Every action turns against you and every word you speak turns against you in a way.

After formal education, I wanted to try my luck in acting and production. It was new for me but for sure I was passionate about it. I used to watch movies and take notes, meet local stage actors and writers, read books and write my ideas. People knew me by my name and I was all set to go. Or so I thought. It turned out that people could work with me but for the project I had to invest a good amount of money. I went to my father and uncles and friends one by one but each time what I received was a refusal wrapped in vivid excuses or explanations. People who knew me for a long time, who were close to me, who had trust in me yet when it came to showing support, they stepped back.

On top of that the producers I met now have dropped a project and moved on to another one. I used to sit outside their office for hours to meet them and even after that what I received was hollow commitment, for sure. "We will let you know for the next project for sure."

I usually get help and advice from Babu but this time I wanted to prove that I was a grown-up man and I could find solutions on my own. With everyone in my life, I was alone.

Babu saw me in this devastating state yet kept calm. Neither she approached me nor gave me any piece of advice. I used to keep quiet while I was at home.

Every morning just like a broker, a hopeless person, I used to take my script and sit at someone's office. If not that, taking naps in the garden at the town's lake was another way to kill my time until the opportunity strikes. I was waiting for a miracle, a change to happen: someone to find me magically, recognizing my talent and handing me a project. I was angry, annoyed and losing hope now.

It was a Friday morning when Babu asked me to take her to the temple. I thought she would show some compassion and would give me her advice and that at that point, I was not in a state to listen to anyone. Not even her. After a 20-minute ride, we reached the less crowded temple. It seemed only a few people were there. Babu, I, Panditji, God, and those ducks catching fish in the lake beside the temple.

While sitting on the floor, by the pillar I saw Babu praying, chanting, and taking some prasad for me. She came and sat beside me, offered me some prasad and kept silent.

I wished she would ask me something so I could take out my anger and frustration on her.

Soon, we got up and stood near the lake watching the birds.

"It seems you have finally found what you want to do in life."

"What? Do not talk about any of it. Nothing is going right."

"Oh. I thought every day you were going out with such passion and power that you must be into something. I thought you must have produced a play or two by now."

She used her taunting tone to annoy me.

If it had not been her, I could have done something to the person who was making fun of my critical situation where my whole career was in jeopardy.

Yet, I kept calm and explained everything to her quickly before I broke into tears.

I cried like a child. I wanted to run away. I wanted to take some action. But I did not know what to do. I was not lazy or stupid Why?

She did not stop me from crying or console me. Instead, she just kept her hand on my head and let my heart empty out.

"Why are things not working out Babu? Have I done anything wrong? No one is supporting me or showing trust in me. People need money for my work. I do not have money, and no one is helping me out."

Young Vivek was now talking to his best friend.

"Do you remember your bicycle?"

"Yes."

"You loved it, right? Wherever you go, you would ride it, cleaning 4 times a day, not letting anyone touch it and decorating it every now and then."

"Hmmm hm"

"And those toys you cried for and stopped eating until your father went and bought for you?"

"Yes. I know. Do you want me to play with them now?"

"Nope."

"Then... come to the point. I am getting late. Do not circle around it."

"From your childhood, we saw you growing, every now and then coming home with some demand and ideas for which you had a temporary passion."

"I was a kid then, Babu. Kids love toys"

"Yes. That is the point. If you received something, you cried, left it, and went to something else to get something new"

"So..."

"But this time you are serious about your career, as even at this breaking point you are not giving it up. I see you struggling, coming home late. I can sense your desperation and frustration from that uncertain halt. There are 'Why me?' thoughts and cussing yourself out loud.

What would one do, Babu? Should I give up and start another job?"

"Nope. Stick to this, Lala. Momentary passion fades away when struggle shows up. I see you love this work. Keep it up. No struggle ever goes unnoticed by the universe. You should carry this on"

"Where to carry it? No one is giving me a break Babu. They need money"

"Do one thing. Tell them that you have a person ready to invest money in the project but you need to confirm that these people are reliable and their work is good. So, for a project or two, work with them. For free. Make your place. Create your needs. Add value to the work. Make efforts and prove to them that you are a skilled person. Then once the time comes, invest money in it"

"That is the question, Babu. Currently there is no one within my reach who can land me some money. I cannot lie to them to get work. In the end, I have to invest in something."

"I am not asking you to lie. You have the investor. I will invest in your project."

"Nope."

"Why?"

"I do not know. You will invest because you love me and you also do not have that much..."

"That is none of your concern. Just do as I say. Join them now, invest once you trust them, learn, read, observe, and thrive. It is simple. If you are serious and dedicated enough, things will work out in your favor.

"I don't know..."

"Do you trust me...?"

"Where did this come from? Of course."

"Then go and try. Leave the rest to the universe."

Following the agreement, we did years back, saying thanks to each other as friends was forbidden. So, I hugged her with a smile on my face and a relieved heart.

Before leaving the temple, as her lesson, we thanked God for giving us such ideas and always showing us the right path and helping us stay on it.

Surprisingly, the team agreed with my terms and we did 2 projects together. Before going and talking to them about the investor, they called me. It turns out that they loved my work, ideas, and creativity and that they wanted me to work on the next project as head and handle the entire team.

"Ohh. Wow. Thank you. What about my project? I can invest."

"Not to worry. We found another investor who liked your project and wanted to initiate the project at once."

Sometimes, all you can say is thank you. When I reached

home, she was sitting on her chair, singing to herself. The moment she looked at me, a bright glow covered her face.

"Are waah. Congratulations Lala."

In a step or two, I reached her. "How did you know? How? I have not told this to anyone."

"Just look at your face. It is glowing with hope..." She chuckled. "...which means you made it."

Everyone in the family was happy with my success and, more than that, with getting me back from the state of despair.

Years later, whenever I think of those events, I understand that sometimes, we only create a huge labyrinth of scrambled thoughts and get into distress. While, in reality, things can be coped with ease.

I understand that only tough times and devotion are able to differentiate the passion from fascination.

While my parents thought that this also could be another temporary attraction to me, they made the right decision to check my devotion to it. That is what Babu found in me and encouraged me to go for it. My first play was sponsored by my family. Maybe that is why it is still so precious to me.

Chapter SEVEN

POSITIVE TEACHING

We still own the house I grew up in. It is a small house accommodating 10 members. Congested yet together. A room and a small kitchen. On the right side of the room, there was a bathroom. On the other side there was a very narrow gully where people used to keep their old furniture or broken household things in the hope of being used in the future. There at the end was an old bicycle. I was small enough to be able to walk in that gully to get the ball we were playing with. There were unfinished walls covered with moss and dew, a dirty smell of wet and rotten wood, leaking pipes, and leftover parts of an old table. There at the end of the gully, was a skeleton of an old bicycle and on top of that was a beehive. I was forbidden to enter the gully for fear of being attacked by the bees, and in case no one else could come and rescue me from there.

One fine day, when someone shot the ball in the air, it went down the gully and hit the beehive. Unaware of this whole event, I rushed in to get the ball, while I was looking for the ball, I heard buzzing and the next moment I was running frantically to get rid of those bees stinging me all over.

I ran out of the house screaming. My whole family rushed out and panicked to see me rolling on the floor. My father and my mother poured buckets of water on me, cleaned me with a cloth and the bees stopped stinging me, leaving me like a boy whose body was covered with tomatoes and cherries.

I cried hysterically. It was so painful and burning all over that I do not even want to remember it.

I was taken to the doctor and given shots and other treatments. Dimple and my mother were sitting by me, looking at me sadly. Dimple was in shock to see me in this condition. We had a strong bond after all.

Well, the next day Babu came back from her one-day visit to a relative and saw me.

"What is this?" She forgot to take off her chappals and dropped the bag containing sweets she bought for me.

"Bees," Dimple replied.

"Gully."

"Yes."

"I have told you not to go in there. Now, look at you. Looking like a monkey. A ghost from another planet."

She was so angry with me that she avoided talking to me and went into the kitchen.

After freshening up, she came to me with a small bowl containing a homemade paste. She carefully applied it all over my body where the bees left their marks.

“Take a rest and do not go out in the wind or sunlight. You will be okay.”

It took me a few days to recover and get my original face back.

Feeling okay, I went to her and said, “I have nothing for the bees Babu. Still, they jumped on me”

“Maybe you did not, but do you remember them asking you the question before they stung you?”

“No. I just went there looking for the ball and trees surrounded me angrily.” I put my point innocently.

“That is the reason people tell others to keep their distance from bees or beehives. They are like that.” Her eyes now fixed on me.

“Hmmm.” I replied and walked back to complete my homework.

Sometimes, I heard Dadaji suddenly snapping at someone.

“I don’t know whether he was abusive or hurt. What I knew was that I had to make my way ahead.

How can he be hurt?

Why did you not fight with him?

Did Dadaji stop everything and become a nice person?

Sometimes, we do not receive the help or love when we require it the most. Sometimes, we have no one to look at.

Sometimes we stop calling for help because no one replied or we stop looking for it because it never showed up.

Or maybe they were too busy screaming and shouting that they never heard someone else replying to them.

Your Dadaji also had a really troubled childhood. When he was a child, he lost his mother and his father was a farm worker.

Just a few days after the death of his mother, his father took him to the farm with him to join work. They used to spend much time working quietly as the wages were very low.

Gradually, he also became another worker like his father. He was also abused, beaten and stayed hungry for days. Used to wear the same clothes for days, sometimes did not bathe for 10 days, eating whatever can be cooked quickly and with fewer ingredients. Now, when he grew up, he wanted to rest properly, to forget about war and its climate, which he felt he deserved.

Now, he was the maid and cook of the house. He was so poor that his heart narrowed, and finally it became so narrow that it was hard for him to be heard.

He was going emotionally extinct.

What he has collected all these years is bad memories, hunger and pain. So whenever he opens his heart or gets into a situation, what comes to him is the same thing he has. When you understand someone and find that whatever they are doing is less intentional and more of their coping system, that is what they have or are aware of.

"Maybe he used to kick someone's bicycle and pick up fights."

Now I understood the reason why she asked me to go and apologize and clear things with that boy who kicked my bicycle that day.

Maybe that is why she asked me to go and apologize to that boy and befriend him.

She was even happy that I gave him a shirt to feel good that I listened to her and not contributing to making another person with bad memories.

That day, everything she learnt from life, she understood that whatever you project or carry or share, if you are hurt from the inside, your words will be hollow. If you are healed and content, even your silence will be praised.

She has developed a mindset leaning towards positivity and values. She did not want to be another version of her own mother. She realized that her mother also treated her the same way she was raised, as there was no one to take a stand or share knowledge. Her mother taught her to keep quiet, keep working, getting beaten up is okayay, being abused is okay, and staying hungry is also ok.

If someone beats you, keep quiet. The moment you speak, they will get angry and will beat you harder. If you keep quiet, they will leave you alone.

Babu understood that she was in the queue but did not remain there forever.

Chapter

EIGHT

FASHION MODEL BABU

In this final chapter, Nanbai, now affectionately known as Dadi, leaves a lasting legacy of love and wisdom. Her unconditional devotion to her family and her teachings of kindness, resilience, and the pursuit of happiness become the guiding principles for generations to come. Dadi's profound impact reminds us of the enduring power of love and the priceless lessons that live on through the hearts of those she touched.

It was mid-2006, when she was losing her health and was not able to take care of herself.

Most of the time she used to sleep or would stand at the window holding the grills as support. She did not like someone to be occupied with her immediately. "I will do things that I still can," she said proudly. Due to heavy medicine doses, her age and loss of energy, she lost sensation in her body. Unable to get up from the bed and go to the bathroom, she was doing everything in the bed. Both my mother and Dimple were her full-time caretakers. Babu was calling Dimple "Maa".

Not because of any side effects or loss of sensation, but because Dimple was taking care of her as a mother would take care of her child with love.

Giving her a bath, listening to her fumbling talks, taking care of her needs. Babu, even at this age, was not giving up.

After Dimple gave her a bath, she would sit in a towel in front of the wardrobe and would pick the best clothes for herself. She was not compromising on that. Getting proper hairstyle, makeup, and adding a little perfume to add more charm to her. At that time, I did not know whether I should laugh or cry.

After getting ready, she used to turn to me carefully and ask me with a gesture, "How am I looking?" her eyes dancing.

"Fashion Model," my reply with a wink, used to make her laugh.

Things sometimes do not go as we wish them to go. We all knew that she would not be with us for long. Yet, hope was high.

One day, while I was working on a project, I received a call from the hospital that she was not well and that I had to get there quickly.

I felt the ground shaking and small, light bubbles twinkling in front of my eyes making everything appear blue.

With a heavy heart, when I reached the hospital, I saw her sitting in bed, with many of my family members around. My uncles, aunts, cousins, and other relatives were there.

“What happened?” I asked my mother.

“She was not able to breathe properly. But after the injections, she is fine now.”

“I was worried. I thought...”

“I know. We will be with her all the time now.”

After a few minutes, sensing that the worst was over, my family left for home leaving me, Dimple, and my mother at the hospital. As we were the team whom Babu wanted there.

She was chewing on some ideas and as soon as we were alone, she called us to share something important, a lesson of life or a secret of hidden treasure.

“When I die...” She stopped at once, finding the anger in my eyes.

“Okay. ‘Whenever I die...’ is not okay now. Not today... not tomorrow... Maybe after 10 years... Okay?” She made sure that I understood what she is willing to share.

“Yes... go on,” I made sure I was on her side now.

“Okay. Whenever I die, firstly, I want my favorite photo to be kept, and not a stupid-looking photo.

I need to look good and cool.”

The photo that she was mentioning was shot for an advertisement for my production house.

It showed a cool and rebellious lady wearing a yellow and red shirt, huge golden chains and rings, and black reflective sunglasses.

"People will laugh at us and many will not approve of it. They will ask to keep the boring photo"

"You are worried about the stupid people I do not even know and are not caring for my last wish" Getting into a character in a moment to get what she wishes was another of her skills.

"Okay. will do. Then..."

"That I like very much. Please. Please. I would love that." The child spoke again.

"Next is..."

"How many wishes are there, babu?" I laughed again

"Last one...", she replied with a cute face.

"... now do not ask to give a party," I jumped with the same curiosity

"Nah. I do not like noise. She has a look of dislike.

"Okay. I always wanted to do this. On the day when people will come to our house to show their condolences and to share the pain of the loss of the loved one... as prasad, give them the orange flavoured tangy candy."

"Oh, people will laugh at us , Babu... is this a joke?"

"Let them. Who is important to you? I who am sharing her last wishes with you or some random people?" She had a point. A valid point.

“I always wanted to see people discussing something serious and sad while enjoying the tangy candy.” She drew a picture in the air for us. “Just imagine... people will be like... Ohh she was a very good lady and was suffering from an illness for a long time and died of it,” while they were enjoying the candy. Imagine that. They will be confused and I will be laughing a lot even after my death.”

That would be fun. You will do it, right?

“Yes, I will do. Monkey.” I promised.

Only a few days after this discussion did she leave us. The word spread and our neighborhood was swarming with people. People I knew and people I never even saw. Everyone she helped in a way or another was there.

After her death, her Dude photo was set for people to give their condolences. Surprisingly, no one made a face or questioned our sanity. People who knew her smiled at the photo and took the candy and sat down to pray. I found a few old ladies discussing her while enjoying that tangy candy.

“You are mischievous.” I chuckled at her photo while going out... “Sweet Mischief.”

What I have understood from her is that we may read hundreds of books, travel thousands of miles, follow strict rituals or belief systems, but touching one’s heart is something one can only achieve by emitting positivity and unconditional love. It is the love that we do not need to go out and find. It is the love that we can give to ourselves and our loved ones.

"He taught us to be sure of ourselves. Know your worth and have faith that whatever happens is for a reason. Whether you can see it or not. That is life. If God wishes us to face things, we are mere humans. Standing upright, facing the obstacles, and making our way out without losing hope or our morals is what one should do."

"And you kept faith in yourself and God."

"I did. I had to. And I am glad about it. I feel good when I see my family happy and content, struggling but not giving up, and earning less but living a confident and moral life."

Chapter NINE

FINAL MOMENTS: HER LAST LESSON OF LOVE

As Babu's health faded and she entered her final days in the hospital, life quietly shifted around her. She was in the ICU, drifting in and out of consciousness, slowly forgetting the world she had built with so much love. There were moments when she looked at familiar faces but could not recognise them. She did not remember her sons, nor her daughters-in-law. Even her closest family members had become strangers to her fading memory.

But destiny saved one final emotional miracle for me.

That night, I reached the hospital carrying food for my mother and Dimple. As I entered the ICU room, Babu slowly opened her eyes. And in that moment — the most painful and precious moment of my entire life — she recognised me.

Her weak voice trembled as she asked,

"Vivek... khana khaya ke nahi?"

("Vivek... have you eaten?")

I could not hold back my tears. She was in unbearable pain, slipping away from the world, forgetting everyone... yet her heart remembered me.

Even in her last breath, her biggest concern was whether I had eaten my dinner.

That night I understood the purest definition of love.

Love is not spoken — it is lived.

Love remembers even when the mind forgets.

Love cares even when the body is failing.

And the last teacher of this truth in my life was my Dadi.

I want every child, every youngster, and every reader to learn what I learned that night. Grandparents are not just elders; they are blessings. They are living libraries of love. They teach without teaching. They leave without leaving.

That was Babu's final gift to me — a lesson I will carry until my last breath.

CONCLUSION: THE CELEBRATION CONTINUES

,Even today, when I close my eyes, I can still see that ICU room — the silence, the machines, the fear... and Babu's soft trembling voice asking if I had eaten. That memory stays with me as the final symbol of her love. It reminds me every day that true love does not demand anything — it only gives. And I hope that through this book, readers, especially the younger generation, feel inspired to hold their grandparents a little closer, to talk to them more, to learn from them, and to treasure the time that life gives.

And as life continued its quiet dance, something beautiful happened...

I found a partner who understands my heart as deeply as Babu once did. Ankita came into my life not just as my wife, but as a gentle companion who carries warmth in her words and strength in her silence. With her, I discovered that love does not come only from the people who raise us — sometimes it arrives later, in the form of someone who chooses us every single day.

And then came **Siya**...

our little world...

our prayer answered...

our smile in human form.

There is something magical about her — the way she looks at me, the way she laughs, the way she tilts her head in curiosity... it all reminds me of Babu. Sometimes, when Siya runs into my arms or plays mischievously, I feel as if life has gently returned Babu to me in another form. As if the universe whispered, *"Here... the love you lost is coming back to love you again."*

We often tell each other that Siya is not just our daughter — she is Babu's soul revisiting our home, the same sparkle in the eyes,

the same innocence, and the same silent wisdom wrapped inside a tiny heartbeat.

Watching her grow has taught me a new kind of gratitude — a gratitude that feels like life has completed a full circle. My first friend in life was my Dadi... and now my daughter has become the new light guiding our days with the same purity.

And so, the celebration continues — not only in memories,

not only in stories,

but in flesh and blood,

in laughter and footsteps,

in Siya's eyes that carry generations of love.

This book began with Babu...

but it finds its true ending in the small hands of my daughter,

who unknowingly carries forward the legacy of love

that started long before she arrived.